ABUNDANT TRUTH INTERNATIONAL MINISTRIES

Kingdom Discipleship Series

# Kingdom Basics 101

*Foundational Studies for Kingdom Living and Service*

Mister Roderick L. Evans

**Published by Abundant Truth Publishing**
P.O. Box 126 * Camden, NC 27921
Phone: 1-877-841-7209 * Fax: 1-877-841-7209
Web: www.abundantpublishing.net
Email: abundantpublishing@gmail.com

Printed U.S.A.

Front & Back Cover Designs by Abundant Truth Publishing
Image by Gerd Altmann from Pixabay

Abundant Truth Publishing is a ministry of Abundant Truth International Ministries. The primary mission of ATI Ministries is to equip the Body of Christ with tools necessary to defend and contend for the truth of the Christian faith. Jesus Christ came to bear witness of the truth and ATI Ministries is a modern-day extension of His commission (John 18:37).

Kingdom Basics 101: Foundational Studies for Kingdom Living and Service
©2025 Abundant Truth Publishing
All Rights Reserved

**ISBN 13:** 978-1-60141-662-9

Unless otherwise indicated, all of the scripture quotations are taken from the *Authorized King James Version* of the Bible. Scripture quotations marked with NIV are taken from the *New International Version* of the Bible. Scripture quotations marked with NASV are taken from the *New American Standard Version* of the Bible. Scripture quotations marked with Amplified are taken from the *Amplified Bible*.

# Contents

Introduction

Section I - Kingdom Personality    1

Chapter 1 – Kingdom Character    7
Parable of Good Samaritan    10
The Beatitudes    12
The Fruit of the Spirit    17
The Way of Love    20

Chapter 2 – Kingdom Conduct    27
The Works of the Flesh    32
Keys to Kingdom Conduct    37
Rewards of Kingdom Conduct    42

Chapter 3 – Kingdom Charisma    47
Possess    51
Ask    52

# Contents(cont.)

| | |
|---|---|
| Believe | 54 |
| **SECTION II – Kingdom Precepts** | 61 |
| **Chapter 4 – Desire of the Kingdom** | 65 |
| God's Desire | 67 |
| Our Desire | 75 |
| **Chapter 5 – Destiny of the Kingdom** | 83 |
| God is a God of Destiny | 85 |
| We are People of Destiny | 90 |
| **Chapter 6 – Discipline of the Kingdom** | 99 |
| Understanding God's Discipline | 101 |

# Contents (cont.)

Submitting to God's Discipline     107

Bibliography     117

# Introduction

Jesus called His followers disciples. A **disciple** is a convinced adherent of a school or individual who accepts and assists in spreading the doctrines of another. A Christian must not only believe on Jesus but be willing to share the faith of Jesus Christ. In order to do this, the believer has to not only understand his role as a disciple but know how to defend his beliefs.

The Kingdom Discipleship Series

explores the biblical truths that should assist the believer in developing as a disciple of Christ. Not only will Christians grow in their walk with the Lord, but their understanding of foundational biblical truths will also expand.

## In this issue

This teaching and study material focuses on three areas of Kingdom living and service. It includes lessons on developing character, understanding God's plan and purpose for your life, and it explores truths for personal and spiritual growth. This material is suitable for Sunday school, small groups, and bible study.

**KINGDOM BASICS 101**

# -Section I-
# Kingdom Personality

Kingdom Discipleship Series

**KINGDOM BASICS 101**

## KINGDOM BASICS 101

This section is about Kingdom Personality. This section is designed to give the believer insight on how to live in the Kingdom of God.

In order to live victoriously and happily in the Kingdom of God, the believer must possess – Kingdom Character, Kingdom Conduct, and Kingdom Charisma. We will briefly define each of these before examining each closely.

KINGDOM CHARACTER –The believer must have the character and mind of

Christ in order to live a life worthy of the Kingdom of Christ.

KINGDOM CONDUCT – The believer must have a lifestyle fitting for the Kingdom of Christ.

KINGDOM CHARISMA – The believer must have the presence, power, and gifts of the Holy Spirit in his life in order to advance in the Kingdom of God.

We should live as if we are in the Kingdom of God. Only then will we prosper and live in victory. For the scriptures say that our citizenship is in heaven (Philippians 3:20 ASV)

**KINGDOM BASICS 101**

## -Chapter 1-
# Kingdom Character
### (Developing the mind and nature of Christ)

# KINGDOM BASICS 101

## KINGDOM BASICS 101

The believer must possess the character of Christ. It has been the plan of God from the beginning to have sons and daughters. Through the new birth in Christ, we now have power to become the sons of God. Christ came to free us from the bondage of sin, not only in our flesh, but also in our spirit and personality.

This means our character: How do we handle people? How do we deal with disappointment? How do we deal with hurts? How do we deal with life's problems?

In our best and worst moments, we must have the character and nature of God in us. We must have Kingdom Character.

**Parable of Good Samaritan – Luke 10:30–37**

Through this well-known parable, we have an example of character worthy of the Kingdom of God. First, he showed mercy and love toward someone who hated him. In addition, he became fully involved with the man by providing for his needs at the inn.

Can we treat someone that hates us with that same kind of compassion? If not, we still have to grow. The Good Samaritan showed strength of character, while the Priest and Levite demonstrated the complete opposite.

Consider these questions:

a) What character strengths does the Samaritan demonstrate?

b) Would you have been the Samaritan or the Priest and Levite?

c) Are there limitations to demonstrating love and concern, even for unbelievers?

## THE BEATITUDES – Matthew 5:3-12

Jesus gives us this list of character traits that every believer should possess. Not only does He give us the traits, but also the reward for having them.

1) Blessed are the poor in spirit. This refers to those that are humble, who rate themselves insignificant before God. The reward is life in the

Kingdom of heaven.

2) Blessed are those who mourn. This refers to the broken hearted, those who are broken before God and have sacrificed their lives for Him. The reward is that God will comfort them. He gives strength to overcome.

3) Blessed are those who are meek. This refers to those who are mild, patient, and long-suffering. The reward is they shall inherit the earth. God will not withhold any good thing from them that love Him (Psalm 84:11). They

shall walk in dominion in the earth.

4) Blessed are those who hunger and thirst after righteousness. This refers to those who desire to be upright and have right standing with God. The reward is that they shall be filled or satisfied. They shall know how to walk worthy of Him.

5) Blessed are those who are merciful. This refers to those who show compassion and forgiveness. The reward is that they shall receive the same in return. Not only from men,

but also from God.

6) Blessed are those who are pure in heart. These are believers who have right motives in life and who see all things through the heart of God.

The reward is that they shall see God. This means they shall see Him, not only in the end, but see Him manifest in their everyday lives also.

7) Blessed are those who have been persecuted and slandered. These are Christians who have suffered and endured wrong for Christ and His

## KINGDOM BASICS 101

kingdom. They have suffered for doing right. The reward is life in the Kingdom of heaven.

At the end of this teaching, Jesus told his listeners to rejoice and be glad. They would have a great reward in heaven.

**Questions:**

1. Is it possible for us to possess all of these traits?
2. What areas are you weak in?
3. What steps can we take to improve our characters?

## THE FRUIT OF THE SPIRIT – Galatians 5:22-23

In his writings, Paul also dealt with Christian character. He reminded us that Christ's character could be formed in us, but it had to be done in the Spirit. God placed His Spirit in us to help us become who we ought to be.

The Spirit of God not only comes with ministries and gifts, but also with the power to change the heart and mind of man to reflect Christ. The fruit of the Spirit are other character traits:

1) Love – We must be governed by compassion. God is love. (I John. 4: 8)

2) Joy – We can experience happiness with contentment.

The Kingdom of God is not meat and drink, but righteousness, JOY, and peace in the Holy Ghost. (Romans 14:17)

3) Peace – We should seek for peace and let God's peace dwell in us in adverse situations. (John 14:27)

4) Patience – We must be able to endure and wait on God. In addition, we are to exercise patience in our daily affairs. (Isaiah 40:31)

5) Kindness – We must be kind to all, displaying the love of the Father. He is our ultimate example of kindness. (Luke 6:35)

6) Goodness – We should strive to display good unto all men, in spite of their actions, in and outside of the Church. (Galatians 6:10)

7) Faithfulness – We must maintain

our faith in God, but God also must find us faithful. (I Corinthians 4:2)

8) Gentleness – We must not deal with people out of a harsh spirit, but from one of care and concern. (Galatians 6:1)

9) Self-Control – We must not only practice self-control when it comes to the flesh, but also in our dealings with others. (James 3:2)

**THE WAY OF LOVE – I Corinthians 13:1-7**

If we are to have the character of

Christ formed in us, we must be governed by love.

Jesus told the Pharisees that the greatest of the commandments was to love God and second to it was to love your neighbor as yourself (Mark 12:30-31). Jesus aid upon these two commandments the whole law rested.

If our motivation is love we will not have to be overly concerned with developing character. When we operate in love, we operate in the nature and character of Christ. Paul gives us a few characteristics of love in I Corinthians 13:4-8 (NIV).

From this, we can see that if we love, we will be the sons and daughters of God.

*Characteristics of Love*

*Love is patient, love is kind. It does not envy, it does not boast, it is not proud. It does not dishonor others, it is not self-seeking, it is not easily angered, it keeps no record of wrongs. Love does not delight in evil but rejoices with the truth. It always protects, always trusts, always hopes, always perseveres.*

We have to work on our areas of weakness. However, we must remember that if we strive to love, we will overcome every weakness in our character and display the nature of Christ.

**Questions:**

1. How can we love in spite of how we are treated?

**KINGDOM BASICS 101**

2. What can we do to develop the fruit of the Spirit in our lives?

3. Is love an emotion or action? Explain.

## KINGDOM BASICS 101

## Notes:

## KINGDOM BASICS 101

**KINGDOM BASICS 101**

-Chapter 2-
# Kingdom Conduct
(Living as Citizens in the Kingdom of Christ)

**KINGDOM BASICS 101**

Every nation, province, country, town, city, and territory has rules and laws governing them. The same is true in the Kingdom of God. God has a standard of living that we, as believers, must live by.

But we must remember that our good works and acts must be a product of Christ's character in us, else our good works will be condemned as the Pharisees' works were by Christ.

After the nature of Christ is in us, we must live according to His standards. We must live by the Spirit and not by the flesh. The only way to have Kingdom Conduct is through the Holy Spirit. Galatians 5:16:

> *This I say, walk in the Spirit, and ye shall not fulfill the lust of the flesh. (KJV)*
>
> *So I say, live by the Spirit, and you will not gratify the desires of the sinful nature. (NIV)*
>
> *But I say, walk and live habitually in the (Holy) Spirit – responsive to and controlled and guided by the*

*Spirit; then you will certainly not gratify the cravings and desires of the flesh- of human nature without God. (Amplified)*

How can we live by and obey the Spirit of God? How can we walk in the Spirit? We are instructed through the Word and by ministers to walk in the Spirit.

It sounds good, but many are unsure of how to do it. First, we must acknowledge and recognize His presence in us. Then, we must respond to His leading and allow Him to control and guide everyday actions.

**Questions:**

1. What is "walking in the Spirit?'

2. How do we learn to walk in the Spirit?

**THE WORKS OF THE FLESH – Galatians 5:20-21**

In order to overcome the flesh, we must be able to recognize its attributes.

1) Adultery

2) Fornication

3) Uncleanness (impurity)

## KINGDOM BASICS 101

4) Idolatry (stubbornness)

5) Witchcraft (rebellion)

6) Hatred

7) Lasciviousness, which is indecency, sensuality

8) Emulations (jealousy)

9) Wrath (fits of rage, outbursts of anger)

10) Strife (selfish ambition)

11) Seditions (dissension and division)

12) Heresies (factions and sects, opinions)

13) Variance (discord)

14) Envyings

15) Murders

16) Drunkenness

17) Revellings

If we are exhibiting any of these traits in our lives, our conduct will not be suitable for Kingdom living. We must not be afraid to say these things are in our flesh. Often times, we want to call these "workings of the flesh" spirits when they are not. They must be crucified.

Read Parable of the Prodigal Son – Luke

15:11-32

Through this parable, we have an illustration of how one can have right character, but wrong conduct. In addition, we discover how one can have right conduct but wrong character (see II Corinthians 7:1).

The son that remained home had the right conduct, but the wrong character. He had the wrong response to his brother returning home, which was fueled by jealousy. He even questioned his father.

**KINGDOM BASICS 101**

Conversely, the son that left had the right character, but wrong conduct. He did wrong, but he had the strength of character to repent and turn. He acknowledged his sin. This led to him correcting the error in his conduct.

**Questions:**

1. What lessons do you think are learned about God in this parable?

2. What attributes of Kingdom Conduct are in the brother?

3. Which traits of Kingdom Character are in the Prodigal Son?

**KEYS TO KINGDOM CONDUCT**

There are three things we must do in order to have Kingdom Conduct: 1) Develop Kingdom Character, 2) Deny the Flesh, and 3) Live by the Spirit.

I.   DEVELOP KINGDOM CHARACTER

In the first chapter of this bool, we discussed Kingdom Character. Without the character of God in you, you will not have the ability to deny the flesh and live by the Spirit. Much of your good works will only come from vain motives. Having His character enables us to have proper conduct.

II.   DENY THE FLESH

The Spirit must govern our actions. We have debated for years about what we can and cannot do as believers. The answer is simple. If your conduct is not going to edify, you may want to abstain from it.

This may range from watching certain television shows to being involved in the wrong conversation. We must remember these exhortations of scripture:

> *All things are legitimate – permissible, and we are free to do anything we please; but not all things are helpful (expedient, profitable, and wholesome). All things are legitimate, but not all things are constructive [to character] and edifying [to spiritual life]. (I Corinthians 10:23 Amplified)*

*For the flesh lusteth against the Spirit and the Spirit against the flesh; and these are contrary one to the other; so that ye cannot do the things that ye would.* (Galatians 5:17)

*All unrighteousness is sin...* (I John 5:17a)

### III. LIVE BY THE SPIRIT

Kingdom Conduct can only come as the result of being yielded to the Spirit of God. We have two forces warring for control in our lives. The flesh versus the Spirit.

Whichever of these two have control in our lives will determine our behavior and conduct in the Kingdom. Consider the following:

**Live in the presence of the Spirit – Galatians 5:16-17**

**Sow to the Spirit – Galatians 6:7-8**

**Crucify the flesh through the Spirit – Romans 8:13**

Again, how do we allow the Spirit of God to have control in our lives? We do this by living in the Spirit, sowing

## KINGDOM BASICS 101

to the Spirit, and crucifying the flesh. If we live in the Spirit, we will have a greater desire for spiritual things.

We sow to the Spirit by reading, praying, and fellowship with others. We crucify the flesh by applying the Word to our lives through the Spirit.

**Questions:**

1. How can we live in the Spirit daily?

2. How do we sow to the Spirit?

3. How can we "crucify" the flesh?

## REWARDS OF KINGDOM CONDUCT

God does not require us to abstain

**KINGDOM BASICS 101**

from evil to deny us pleasure or happiness. He does it so that He can pour His blessings upon us. There are five rewards for us living holy lives.

They are listed for us on the following pages. Look up the scriptures beside each.

1) Healing - I Chronicles 7:14

2) Answered Prayer - John 15:7

3) Peace - John 14:27

4) Long-life - Psalm 91:15-16

5) Everlasting life - I John 3:3

**KINGDOM BASICS 101**

We have to strive for Kingdom Conduct at all costs. Though trials, tests, and temptations abound, God gives us the necessary tools to achieve proper conduct.

**KINGDOM BASICS 101**

## Notes:

**KINGDOM BASICS 101**

## -Chapter 3-
# Kingdom Charisma
(Possessing the power and presence of the Christ's Spirit)

# KINGDOM BASICS 101

The Old and New Testament both agree that God's desire is for man to be indwelt by his Spirit The Holy Spirit not only helps us to demonstrate the nature of God, but also His power.

God has destined for the believer to walk in power. We can triumph over the enemy through the power that God has promised us (Acts 1:8). What is this power? It is the power and presence of the Holy Ghost.

The plan of God for believers was not that they only possess the character and conduct of Christ, but also His charisma.

When we speak of charisma, we mean gifts. Charisma ('chrisma') was the Greek term Paul used to describe the gifts of the Spirit listed in I Corinthians 12.

Therefore, we must possess character, conduct, and charisma – that is the power and gifts of the Holy Spirit.

In this section, we will deal with what we must do in order to possess the power, presence, and gifts of the

Holy Spirit in our lives.

There are three things we must do in order to possess Kingdom Charisma. They are as follows:

1) Possess

2) Ask

3) Believe.

**I. POSSESS**

What do we need for the presence and power of the Holy Spirit to remain present in our lives? We must have Kingdom Character and Conduct. This is the first step in having the power and gifts of the Spirit manifest in your life consistently.

God is first concerned with our lifestyles and then with giving us power and gifts. If you strive for His nature and character, His presence and power will be yours to ask for.

## II. ASK

As we strive to live as God commands us to, we must then ask for the Holy Spirit and His power. Though He is our Father and He loves us, we must seek after His presence. Read

Parable of the friend in need – Luke 11:5-13

Jesus always used parables to explain spiritual things. This parable teaches us a few things:

1) God will not give to us just because of our relationship with Him. The man did not rise because they were friends. He got up because of his persistence. God wants us to be persistent in our asking.

2) It is His will to give to us more of the presence and power of the Spirit.

After this parable, Jesus said that God WILL give the Spirit to those who ask for it.

3) We must ask, seek, and knock until we get a response. If we will be unwavering in our asking, we will receive.

## III. BELIEVE

We must learn to move and operate in faith with spiritual matters. Many people have the gifts of God in them and are afraid to use them because of doubt.

**KINGDOM BASICS 101**

After asking and seeking God for His presence, power, and gifts, we must move in faith and become His channels. Consider the following:

*And these signs shall follow them that believe; In my name shall they cast out devils; they shall speak with new tongues; they shall take up serpents; and if they drink any deadly thing, it shall not hurt them; they shall lay hands on the sick and they shall recover. (Mark 16:17-18)*

## KINGDOM BASICS 101

also,

> *As every man hath received the gift, even so minister the same one to another as good stewards of the manifold grace of God. (I Peter 4:10)*

After God has blessed us, we should allow His signs to follow us. After we have received whatever gifts He has bestowed upon us, we must minister to others what we have received.

Study the following passages

## KINGDOM BASICS 101

concerning gifts and ministries. They will prepare you for the Chapters on the gifts and ministries:

ROMANS 12:5-8

I CORINTHIANS 12:1-10

I CORINTHIANS 12:28

-see also Ephesians 4:11

**Questions:**

1. What three steps are needed to possess Kingdom Charisma?

2. What three things do we learn about asking from the Parable of the friend in need?

**KINGDOM BASICS 101**

3. Has fear caused you not to trust God's gifts in you?

**KINGDOM BASICS 101**

# Notes:

**KINGDOM BASICS 101**

# -Section II-
# Kingdom Precepts

As believers, we can know the plan of God. Even with this, many believers are confused and do not understand the dealings of God in their lives. It is our intent in the section to examine the purpose of God in our lives.

**KINGDOM BASICS 101**

**KINGDOM BASICS 101**

God has a plan for believers. He orchestrates all of the events in our lives. He has a specific goal in mind for each of us.

Many of the circumstances that occur in our lives are to get us into the perfect will of God. We will examine three areas that God is concerned with.

KINGDOM DESIRE – God has a desire to produce sons and daughters in the Kingdom. We must develop the desire to become sons and daughters.

**KINGDOM BASICS 101**

KINGDOM DESTINY – God has a specific destiny for each of us in the Kingdom. We must strive to fulfill our God-given destiny.

KINGDOM DISCIPLINE – God has to discipline us in order to cause us to fulfill His desire and our destiny. We must submit to the discipline of God.

Through examining these three areas, we can develop a mind to understand and fulfill our purpose in the Kingdom.

**KINGDOM BASICS 101**

-Chapter 4-
# Desire of the Kingdom

**KINGDOM BASICS 101**

**KINGDOM BASICS 101**

## I. GOD'S DESIRE

God has a plan and purpose for our lives. God orchestrates the events in our lives. No circumstance ever comes upon us without God having prior knowledge. He has control over the situations in our lives, even those that are adverse. We should realize that God has desires even as we have desires.

To "desire" means to wish or long for. It also means to want strongly. What is it that God longs for and wants strongly? He desires for us to become sons and daughters, to be just like His only begotten Son Jesus. More than anything else, God wants us to become like Him.

> *For whom he did foreknow, he also did predestinate to be conformed to the image of his Son, that he might be the firstborn among many brethren. (Romans 8:29)*

Believers consistently wonder what God has for them to do. He wants you to become like Jesus. After the work of Christ on the cross, God sent His Spirit to dwell in man.

The Spirit came to give us power and to make us the children of God. Let us now look at some scriptures to show this.

THE GOAL IS SONSHIP, NOT MINISTRY!!!!!

(Our goal should be to become his children, not just to posses His power)

1) The indwelling Spirit comes to make us sons.

*He predestined us to adoption, as sons through Jesus Christ to Himself, according to the kind intention of His will. Ephesians 1:5*

God places His Spirit in us to make us partakers of His divine nature. The indwelling of the Spirit is the same as parents signing adoption papers for a child. The Spirit knows what is the mind of the Father; that is, to make the children of men, the sons of God.

2) The Spirit causes us to recognize God as our Father.

*For ye have not received the spirit of bondage again to fear; but ye have received the Spirit of adoption, whereby we cry, Abba, Father. Romans 8:15*

Jesus told the Pharisees that their father was the devil. He wanted them to know that they were not the sons of God though they were Abraham's children. The Holy Spirit comes to help us recognize and receive God as our

Father.

3) Jesus is our example and big brother.

> *For both he that sanctifieth and they who are sanctified are all of one: for which cause he is not ashamed to call them brethren, Saying, I will declare thy name unto my brethren, in the midst of the Church will I sing praise unto thee. Hebrews 2:11-12*

God sent Jesus into the world to be an example to us of how we should live. He said that we should follow Him. We follow Him by emulating Him. He is the first born among men brethren (Romans 8:29).

4) Since we are Christ's brethren, we are joint-heirs with him.

*And because ye are sons, God hath sent forth the Spirit of his Son into your hearts, crying, Abba, Father. Wherefore thou art no more a servant, but a son, and if a son, then an heir of God through*

## KINGDOM BASICS 101

*Christ. Galatians 4:6-7*

Paul tells us in his writings that they were heirs in the Kingdom of God. An heir is usually a son or daughter. We are called joint- heirs. This means when Christ comes into His Kingdom, we will be a part of it also.

5) We will be sons in this life and in the life which is to come.

*Beloved, now are we the sons of God, and it doth not yet appear what we shall be: but we know when he shall appear we shall be like him, for we shall see him as he is. I John 3:2*

The ultimate plan of God is for us to be His children for all eternity. Even when this mortal life is over, we will be sons and daughters in the Kingdom of God.

## II. OUR DESIRE

Our desire must mirror God's desire. Since God's ultimate desire for us is to become sons and daughters, our desire should be to become sons and daughters. Our goal should be to reach maturity in Him. There are five things necessary to become like Christ and to be His children:

1) We must LOVE in order to be like Him. One of the greatest signs to the world that we are His children is love.

> *And thou shalt love the Lord thy God with all thy heart, and with all thy soul, and with all thy mind, and with all thy strength; this is the first commandment. Mark 12: 30.*

2) We must PRESS to be like Him. We must have endurance and stamina in our walk with God. Without the desire to press, we will be stunted in our growth and development in Him.

*I press toward the mark for the prize of the high calling of God in Christ Jesus. Philippians 3:14 {see also Luke1:32, 76}*

3) We must FOLLOW Christ's example. We need to emulate Christ's actions. His standard for living must become our standard.

**KINGDOM BASICS 101**

*For I have given you an example that ye should do as I have done to you. John 13:8*

4) We must DEVELOP His mind. Not only must we imitate His actions, there must be a change in our attitudes and thoughts.

*Let this mind be in you, which was also in Christ Jesus. Philippians 2:5*

5) We must OBEY and become the Word. Our lives are to become a living demonstration of the Word.

**KINGDOM BASICS 101**

*But be ye doers of the word, and not hearers only... James 1:22*

*And the word was made flesh, and dwelt among us. John 1:14a*

**Questions:**

1. How do we develop a desire to become like Christ when we are facing so many other concerns in life?

2. Why do you think God's desire is for us to His children?

3. What role does the Holy Spirit play in us becoming sons and daughters?

**KINGDOM BASICS 101**

## Notes:

**KINGDOM BASICS 101**

**KINGDOM BASICS 101**

-Chapter 5-

# Destiny of the Kingdom

# KINGDOM BASICS 101

**KINGDOM BASICS 101**

## I. GOD IS A GOD OF DESTINY

God has a plan for each of our lives. Though His ultimate desire is for us to become sons and daughters, He has also placed us in the earth to reach a certain destiny. God is a God of purpose.

Everything that He does has a reason and purpose behind it. If God has allowed us to live thus far, it is because we have not reached our destiny. God has a predetermined will for your life.

## KINGDOM BASICS 101

It is His desire for us to fulfill the purpose He has for our lives. You do not have to worry about missing Him. When it is your time, God will make His plan clear to you. Remember these five facts about the plan and destiny of God for your life:

1)  God's plan for your life is settled. Even before we knew God, He had already declared what we are to do in Him. Regardless of mistakes and failures, God's plan does not change.

## KINGDOM BASICS 101

*Declaring the end from the beginning, and from ancient times the things that are not yet done, saying, My counsel shall stand, and I will do all of my pleasure. Isaiah 46:10*

2) God's destiny for you was established before you were born. He told Jeremiah that before he was conceived, his destiny was established.

*Before I formed thee in the belly I knew thee; and before thou camest forth out of the womb I sanctified thee, and I ordained thee a prophet unto the nations.* Jeremiah 1:5

3) God's plan for your life is beyond your imagination. There are individuals whom God has great plans for, but their faith is small. They forget that God does not think like us, nor does he see us the way we see ourselves.

*For my thoughts are not your thoughts, neither are your ways my ways, saith the Lord. For as the heavens are higher than the earth, so are my ways higher than your ways, and my thoughts than your thoughts. Isaiah 55:8-9*

4) God's destiny for you is good. Believers have to resist the temptation to feel that the only plan that God has for them is to suffer. Though God is glorified in our suffering, He is also glorified in our prosperity.

*For I know the plans that I have for you, declares the Lord, plans to prosper you and not to harm you, plans to give you a hope and a future. Jeremiah 29:11 NIV*

5) God's plan for you will come to pass. The very thoughts of God will happen. He is more than able to perform His Word in you.

*The Lord of hosts hath sworn, saying, surely as I have thought, so shall it come to pass and as I have purposed, so shall it stand. Isaiah 14:24*

## II. WE ARE A PEOPLE OF DESTINY

The plan of God for our lives is settled. Though this is true, many are still ignorant of the will of God. They do not realize that once they enter into the Kingdom of God, they become a people of destiny.

We must remember that we can only fulfill our destiny through and in Him. We must become a destiny-minded people and go toward the perfect will of God for our lives. But in order to reach our destiny, there are five practical steps to be followed:

1) In order to reach our destiny we must FORGET the former things. We

cannot allow the failures and mistakes of the past to dictate our future. Even if we have made mistakes, we can still fulfill the plan of God.

> *Brethren, I count not myself to have apprehended: but this one thing I do, forgetting those things, which are behind, and reaching forth unto those things, which are before. Philippians 3:13*

2) In order to reach our destiny we must KNOW the will of God. No one can do His will except it is known. If you

do not know what God has for you, ask until you get an answer.

> *Wherefore be ye not unwise, but understanding what the will of the Lord is. Ephesians 5:17*

3) In order to fulfill our destiny we must BELIEVE. After discovering the will of God, faith must be applied. There are Christians that know what their destinies are, but they do not believe they can do it. Remember, we live and walk by faith.

> *But Jesus beheld them, and said*

*unto them, with men this is impossible, but with God all things are possible. Matthew 19:2*

*Jesus said unto him, If thou canst believe, all things are possible to him that believeth. Mark 9:23*

4) In order to reach our destiny we must PREPARE ourselves. With every job and occupation, there are required skills. They are certain things we must do in order to fulfill the will of God; namely, prayer and study of the Word.

*But we will give ourselves continually to prayer, and to the ministry of the Word. Acts 6:4*

5) We can FULFILL our God-given destiny. Paul told Timothy that he finished his course. This means that he finished the course God had for him in ministry. Pray and ask God to allow you to finish your course also.

*I have fought a good fight, I have finished my course, I have kept the faith. I Timothy 4:7*

## KINGDOM BASICS 101

**Questions:**

1. What is your God-given destiny or purpose?

2. What is hindering you from fulfilling your destiny?

3. What steps can you take to overcome these hindrances?

4. What steps do you need to take now in order to reach your destiny?

5. Do you want to fulfill your destiny while on the earth?

## KINGDOM BASICS 101

# Notes:

**KINGDOM BASICS 101**

**KINGDOM BASICS 101**

-Chapter 6-
# Discipline of the Kingdom

# KINGDOM BASICS 101

## I. UNDERSTANDING GOD'S DISCIPLINE

No one likes to be corrected or disciplined. We call God our Father. If He is a Father, He will deal with us as a father would his children. This means that God will discipline us.

In Chapters 7 and 8, we discovered that God's ultimate desire is for us to be His children and that He has a specific destiny for each of us. Because God wants us as children and wants us to fulfill destiny, He disciplines us so that

**KINGDOM BASICS 101**

we will not miss His blessing, or our purpose.

Discipline means training that teaches one to obey rules and control his behavior. Is this not what God does with us as believers?

He allows circumstances and situations to happen in our lives to teach and train us. Let us remember the following factors concerning God's discipline:

ALL ADVERSE SITUATIONS ARE NOT CAUSED BY THE DEVIL!!!!

## KINGDOM BASICS 101

1) God's discipline does not always come as the result of sin.

*Every branch in me that beareth not fruit he taketh it away: and every branch that beareth fruit, he purgeth it, that it may bring forth more fruit. John 15:2*

When a tree is pruned, its branches are clipped. It is left bare in order to bear more fruit. If you are fruitful in the Kingdom of God, you will also be pruned. God does this so that you will bring forth more fruit.

2)   God's discipline comes to cause us to cease from sin.

> *For they verily for a few days chastened us after their own pleasure; but he for our profit, that we may be partakers of his holiness. Hebrews 12:10*

God disciplines us that we may stop our sinful acts. He demands holiness from His people. God is holy and we have to be holy. He has called us to walk in His holiness.

3) God's discipline comes as a result of His love toward us.

*As many as I love, I rebuke, and chasten: be zealous therefore, and repent. Revelation 4:19*

When God disciplines us, it is not born out of anger, but love. An earthly parent chastises their child in order to protect them. God disciplines us so that we will not have to be judged with the world.

4) God's discipline comes to save us.

*He that overcometh, the same*

*shall be clothed in white raiment; and I will not blot out his name out of the book of life, but I will confess his name before my Father, and before his angels. Revelation 3:5*

He chastises us so that He will not have to destroy us. He protects us from His wrath by His discipline.

God's discipline comes to save us. Christ died to grant us salvation. His discipline comes so that we will keep it.

5) God's discipline is just.

*Yet you say, the way of the Lord is not just. Hear, O house of Israel: Is my way unjust? Is it not your ways that are unjust? Ezekiel 18:25 (NASV)*

We can be assured that His discipline is just. God will never discipline prematurely or without cause.

## II. SUBMITTING TO GOD'S DISCPLINE

God disciplines us because He loves us and He does not want us to miss the things that He has prepared for us. Often times, the believer is confused about what is going on in his life and ends up fighting against God rather than working with Him. If we are to prosper and mature in God, we must be able to endure His discipline. Submitting to God's discipline brings great blessing. Consider the following:

1) Submitting to God's discipline demonstrates relationship.

> *If ye endure chastening, God dealeth with you as sons; for*

*what sons he whom the father chasteneth not. Hebr. 12:7*

When God disciplines us, He is affirming to us that we are His children. If God chastises you, it should comfort you. It lets you know that God is still interested in you and your well-being.

2) Submitting to God's discipline brings power and authority.

*Submit yourselves therefore unto God. Resist the devil and he will flee from you. James 4:7*

The authority we have over the enemy is proportionate to how we submit ourselves to the discipline of God. After we are submitted to God, we will have the power to resist the devil.

3) Submitting to God's discipline brings the flesh under control.

> *Forasmuch then as Christ hath suffered in the flesh, arm yourselves likewise with the same mind: for he that has suffered in the flesh hath ceased from*

*sin. I Peter 4:1*

God will allow us to suffer. The suffering comes to get our attention away from fleshly desires. When this is accomplished, we will forget those sins that easily entrap us.

4) Submitting to God's discipline brings His blessings.

*...let him alone, and let him curse; for the Lord hath bidden him. It may be that the Lord will look on mine affliction and that the Lord will requite me good for his*

*cursing this day. 2 Samuel 16:11-12*

David realized that if he allowed himself to be humbled, God might bless him. God may allow adverse situations so that He can bless us. If we humble ourselves when He disciplines, we are sure to reap the benefits.

5) Submitting to God's discipline reverses His judgment.

> *Repent; or else I will come unto thee quickly, and will fight against them with the sword of my mouth. Revelation 2:16*

**KINGDOM BASICS 101**

The Church at Pergamos was filled with error. God was ready to judge her. God still gave them another chance. He told them that if they repent, He would not have to judge her. The same applies to us. If we repent, God will change His mind concerning us.

**Questions:**

1. Has God ever disciplined you? How did you handle God's discipline?
2. Can you discern between God's discipline and an attack of the enemy? If so, explain.

3. How should we view God's discipline?

**KINGDOM BASICS 101**

# Notes:

**KINGDOM BASICS 101**

# Bibliography

Smith, William. Smith's Bible Dictionary. Holman Bible Publishers. Nashville, Tennessee. c1994

The Bible Library. The Bible Library CD Rom Disc. Ellis Enterprises Incorporated, (c) 1988n 2000. 4205 McAuley Blvd., Suite 385, Oklahoma City, OK 73120. All Rights Reserved.

**KINGDOM BASICS 101**

Lockman Foundation. Comparative Study Bible. Zondervan Publishing House. Grand Rapids, MI, c1984

**KINGDOM BASICS 101**

## Notes:

_____

_____

_____

_____

_____

_____

_____

_____

**KINGDOM BASICS 101**

www.ingramcontent.com/pod-product-compliance
Lightning Source LLC
Chambersburg PA
CBHW050342010526
44119CB00049B/658